Notes on Hell

T Abbott Collins

FIFTH ENTELECHY PUBLISHING

"Dinosaur Arithmetic," "Ghost Symmetry," "Naked Homer," and "Technicolor" were first published in *The Waggle*, October 2014.

"Desertion" and "Vertigo" were first published in *The Quint*, Volume 6 Issue 4 September 2014.

"Condemned," "Detheburgher," "Opera Eulogy," and "Trembled" were first published in *BlazeVOX*, Fall 2015.

All images are AI generated and copyrighted by the author.

T Abbott Collins/Fifth Entelechy Publishing
fifthentelechy@gmail.com
Buffalo, NY/14214

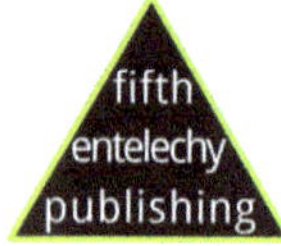

Book Layout © 2017 BookDesignTemplates.com

Notes on Hell/ T Abbott Collins -- 1st ed.
ISBN 979-8-9910063-2-3

Contents

Through the Wood	1
Doing It Right	2
That Furnace	3
Talking Statues	4
Dinosaur Arithmetic	5
snakes of course	6
Incomprehensible	7
Technicolor	8
seven-year-old poet	9
Maddog	10
Old Man Indian	11
Beacon	12
On Neptune	14
Trembled	15
Greek Bebop	16
Jeopardy	17
The Other Place	19
Dark Cyborg	20
Courteous Pain	21
Behind the Altar	23
Jugular	25
Waiting for the Flood	26

The Dog Drinks   27

Skyline   28

More Than Your Will   29

first-century christian martyr   30

Panic   32

Bridge in the Flood   33

Opera Eulogy   34

Penance and Unpeace   36

Form Divine   38

Stoic Postured   39

Ani Anam Ra   40

Alchemical Premise   41

Cascade   42

Wander Still   43

The Station   45

Pull the Strings   47

Vertigo   49

What Is Prayer   50

What Is Poetry   51

Detheburgher   53

Naked Homer   54

Venusian Ovens   55

Good Old Orc   56

Before They Spoke   57

Black Crystal Foliage   59

Desertion   60

Make You Stop	61
More Climes	62
From the Starship	63
Ghost Symmetry	64
Bad Epiphanies	65
Like Neuroses	67
Tentacles	68
Was Real	69
Soothsayer	70
Avoiding Destruction	72
Blue-assed Baboon	73
A Flag of Vision	74
Our Lady	76
Diagrams	77
Organic Arpanet	78
Weird Arena	79
Far Gone	80
Burnished Arm	81
A New Scourge	82
Condemned	83
Eclipse	84
Same Bloody Sun	85
Water Hydraulics	86
Blue Christmas Lights	87

Notes on Hell

⊕

T Abbott Collins

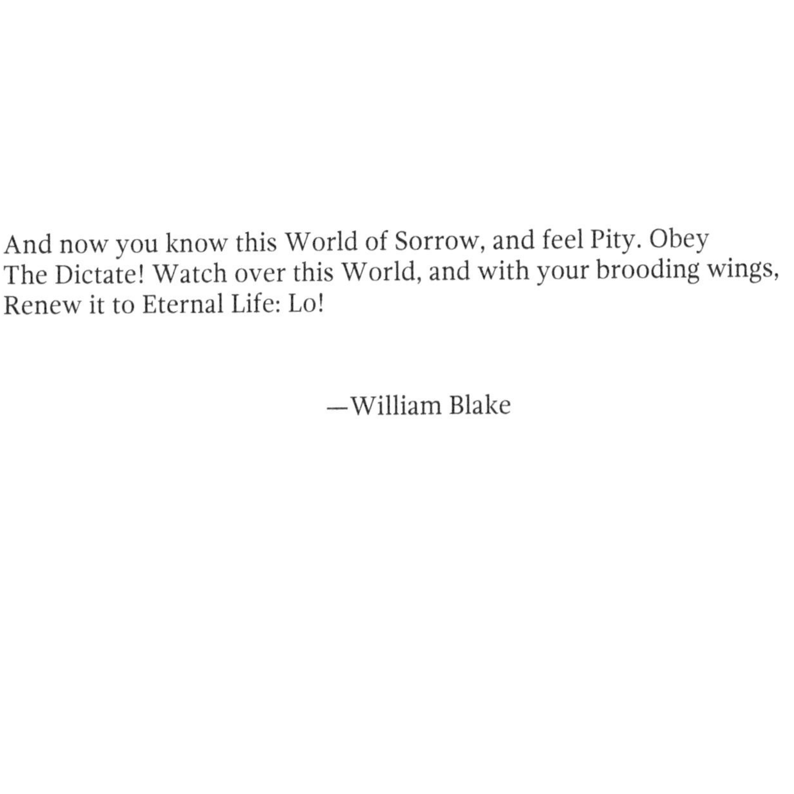

And now you know this World of Sorrow, and feel Pity. Obey
The Dictate! Watch over this World, and with your brooding wings,
Renew it to Eternal Life: Lo!

—William Blake

Through the Wood

"the indians made me do it"

it's only
you don't talk
too much —

we've trudged through
a lot of wood
      together
my friend

strangled by ideals
and not knowing
how to survive

the seven horrors
of the Holy Ghost

hell-shock treatments

nebular roller coaster
forgot the cure exists

the peace of reaching
the new plateau —
      misty seasons

Doing It Right

hurt myself
trying to find
the doorknob
in the dark —

(otherside of the tunnel
life served on a platter)

only hurt
cause you were
doing it right

she falls asleep
I slip back —
get to the border
she turns around

I recorded
every ray
of sunlight

That Furnace

shortcuts take longer

last battle
(or bottle)
of the sea on
fire they're
holding the note
of tension an
extra bar

set free in time
yet hostage of space

let's see how far
we can push the
human mold
in that furnace

stranded at the vigil they
already read our fate

shadows in the West is
that dawn or is it night

baby wolf fangs
home in on the break

Talking Statues

you can see the
wind when kids
arrive with spurts
of blood and you're
slapped with mutinous
delirium —

        luck and fate
        and dementia
        and scars

the alchemist
sets aside
youth to consummate
wisdom with
talking statues

it's OK to
milk the clay

Dinosaur Arithmetic

sovereign poems
make an image
for everything

I'd like to say
dinosaur
one more time

St. Thomas

tried to will
the dawn with
arithmetic —
it almost worked

all this exhausting
care and it's just
a trick of the light

snakes of course

the Ancients spoke
through our wounds

to experience life
as deeply as
it can be and
wonder why —

weeds that grow
in the chasm of
the broken heart,
snakes of course

is loneliness

the hills blanketed
in their blue
tumescent radiation

I was ready
the wind
was putrid

the soul doesn't
transgress just
another round of
catatonic despair

Incomprehensible

symmetry funneling
infinity through the
present and plumed
Destiny flapping in
black waters of time

magnetic wind
storms keep the
solitude going the
mind desperate

too hardened for
the giddy sleep

watching the world
from afar resigned
to some incomprehensible
vengeful innocence

sharks stalk him
waiting for the light

Technicolor

the struggle
of sowing
the seed
the steering
of the ship

metamorphoses

when I see
myself
reflected back
from the
skyline

all the way
back to mortality
in sad
technicolor

seasoned with fire
love the night

seven-year-old poet

the seven-year-
old poet dreaded
the naked beggar
Homer bailing
out in the streets

"where did this drunken fucking
monster come from?"

says the boy

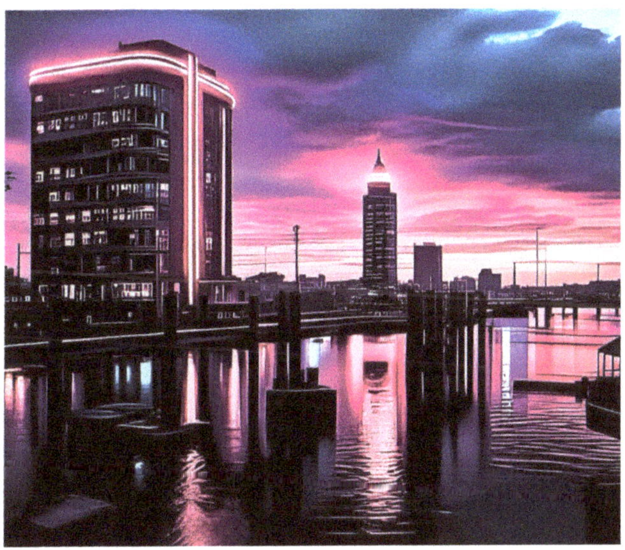

Maddog

she asked me "what
is it why do I
feel this way!" as
the Goddess begins
to rustle in the
compost heap

        pirate signals
        unified symbols
        maddog on the
        border town

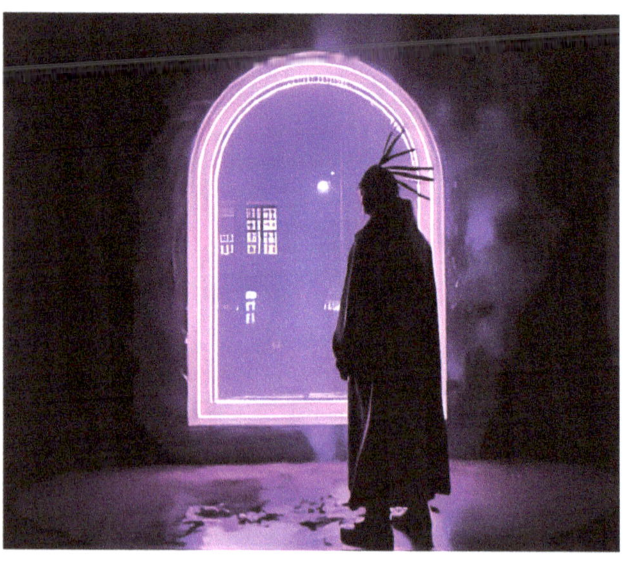

Old Man Indian

I'm an ancient landmark
to the waking world —
the door is open
it stopped raining so
I went back to bed

the Old Man Indian
        KNEW
giggling in his clay

in serving "god"
god knows all
        brilliance
            and
none of the flesh

guarding the Tree
severed of connection

ghostship with a leak
in the window
of the chamber

the performers are
coolly entrenched
around the
pit of fire

Beacon

the violence of formation —
2

pure contemplation
lets the clay figurine
go to utter hell

anything spoken
not One Voice
filled my brainpan
with images of
concentration camps
and nuclear holocaust

"saw a Shakespearean
rape scene in NYC"

lift my head
out of the shell
and wisely say
"I'm only schizo
cause you are"

master of epilepsy
nervous breakdown
beacon of light

I already know
all the pagan stories

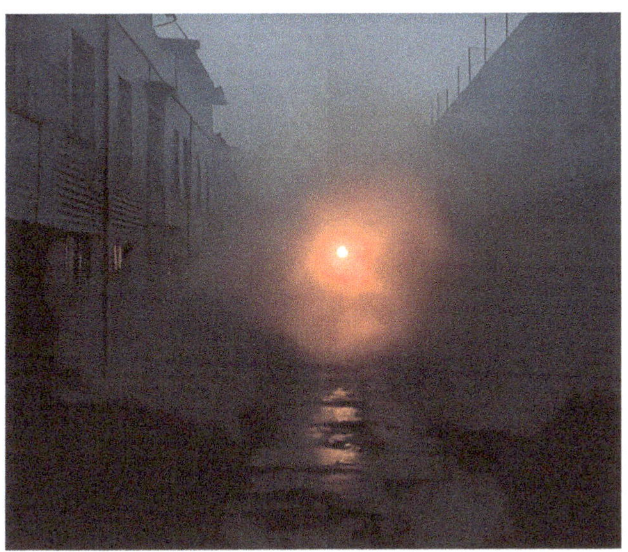

On Neptune

they call it being
dead on Neptune
Elsinore's black
hills chattering

cool kids lament
from the balcony
while I gnash
disembodied
deaf & dumb

    "through this tunnel
        of dementia
   we re-emerge
      in infancy"

Trembled

there were holocausts
in Africa maybe that
was it that night at
the carnival the air
           trembled

where have the gypsies
gathered in this life

infinitely misunderstood

I want the music to
take me to the arctic
        dream chamber

swinging off the power
lines like ski lifts

Greek Bebop

"What did they do to you? This
can't happen to him! Who did
this to you?"

she said

as he oozes back
into the exiled
jelly fish gutter corpse

"I didn't know this happens!
Nobody knows this happens!"

Story of the Ages
Greek Bebop in Blue

"They have removed
my Lord and I
know not where to
find him!" she said
"Where is he!"

Jeopardy

bitter shaman
in the moat
with the goat

    "I guess when I whore
      myself this occult wisdom
      will do me some good
      finally"

devoured by darkness
surrounded no surrender
the spirit saved him
and put me in jail

poor lonely Adam
destined to lay around
ridiculously without
deliverance of the flesh

depraved monster
feeling open
the rubber
cocoon hymen

tantric celibacy
unconscious alchemy
metaconception

waiting for the room
to stop spinning
the end or beginning
whenever Love's
not in jeopardy

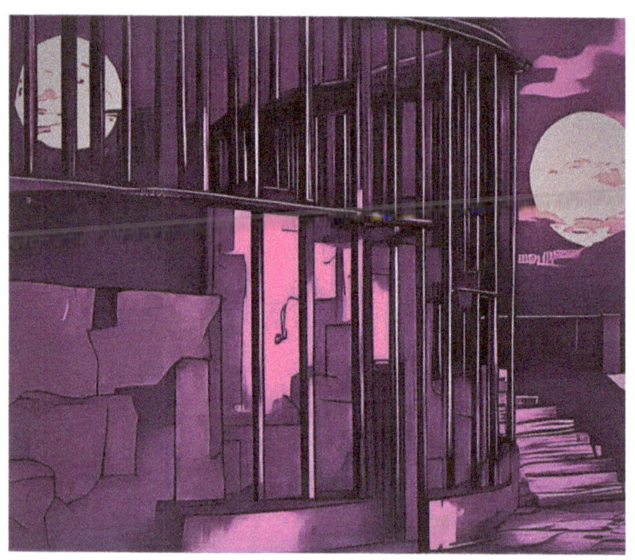

18

The Other Place

aren't we born
to muse & gesture,
dream, from this
forgotten outpost

"you masochist
fucking freak"

hard times

the drama
the drama
the comedy

bangladesh
strangled dress
aboriginee

time to go to
the other place

Dark Cyborg

Roman Arabic

get fucked with

"Lord knows
we all have
short memories"

Phoenician Venetian

third world mentality
when I need
a meager donation

paranoia's just
bad sound control —
dark cyborg
of sensation

Courteous Pain

plenty of people have magic

struggling and suffering
to maintain One Voice

visitation

drunken schizo
Buddha Master
morbidly alone
and groaning

    "once again
      all we have
      is you know
      whatever"

I wish an angel
were here to watch
me hanging on
exhausted from
the massacre

      lays down his head
      lets the storm clouds
      pass safe enough
      here down in the hole

the courteous pain
of desolation
peering through
the crack
in my door

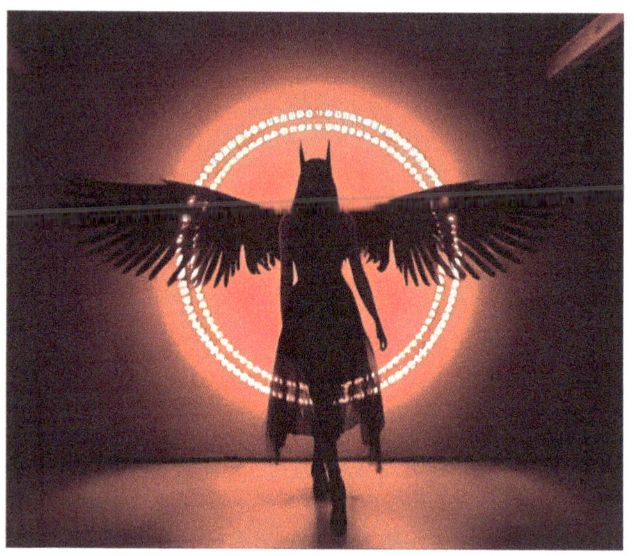

Behind the Altar

Magdelena

keeper
of my bones

black wings descending
from the underbelly
of a lighted candle

      &

the gravitational parallax
of the underground sun

      satyr wrapped in
      sheep skins
      incandescent fox eyes
      prowl in the shadows

      "the ghosts keep saying
      how hard they worked
      to haunt me and when
      I awake from this
      monstrous sleep and
      return to Life &
      Time & Self they'll
      be dead on the
      ashes of my cigar"

these tempests
of memory
& lethargy
blood letting
to purify
the sacrifice

we belong behind the
altar or in the clouds
with sacramental wine

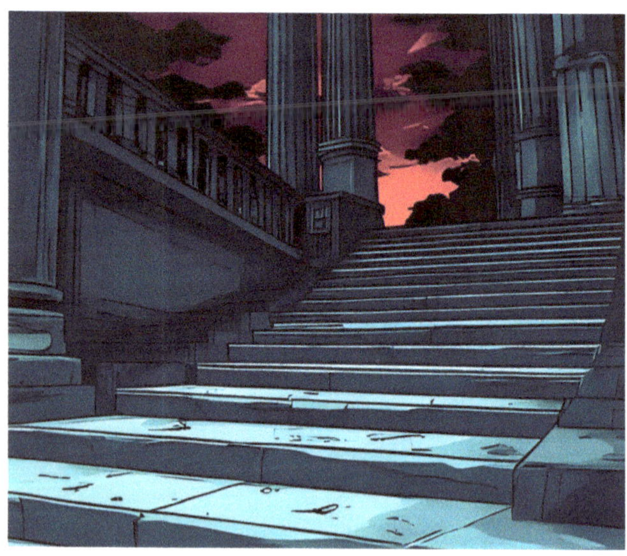

Jugular

on limestone
stairs prayer
navigates the
dark wood

elliptical progress
transcending demons

slowly flesh
germinates on
the skeleton

"binge on that poison:
it's good for your jugular"

getting back we
were amazed
it didn't hurt —

receive communion
through the
page or speaker

Waiting for the Flood

for how many generations

somehow evolutionary byproduct
    obtained the reins
    which can't be taken
    in a day

hungover
    & waiting for the Flood —

what else is there to say

you must be bored
for so long

that's the dream

The Dog Drinks

she rejected the worship so
off to the catacombs to learn
the alchemy of torch bearing
with debauchery and mourning
the phantom wife smiled
from on high as he
held the pot on a hill

the dog
drinks to
his health

"what is this
sick struggle?"

"Fame on our tombstone
against your will"

Skyline

the ghost ship
falls over
the waterfall
and there are
blizzards
on the sun

our image in Time
painful progress

the Light when
I see myself
reflected in
the skyline

More Than Your Will

"why did you
lock yourself
in the bunker
after the war
was over?"

"takes more
than your will
to give up
this ghost. do
you think this
grief is going
to assuage
itself?"

laps of purgatory

the dog works on
his own clock
whetting his appetite

but I'm in love with
this strange delusion

first-century christian martyr

I already know all
the pagan stories —

citizens of the domain

innocence is shame
              &
you're unchanged

"you see in Egypt somehow
the royal lineage was broken
and in Rome the Neanderthals
managed to elbow their way
into political autonomy, so by
the time Christ got to the Jews . . ."

"give me industrial
strength paint thinner"
says the first-century
christian martyr —

"eject from pyromaniac blimp!"

coming alive
to the music

listen to
the foliage
rustle

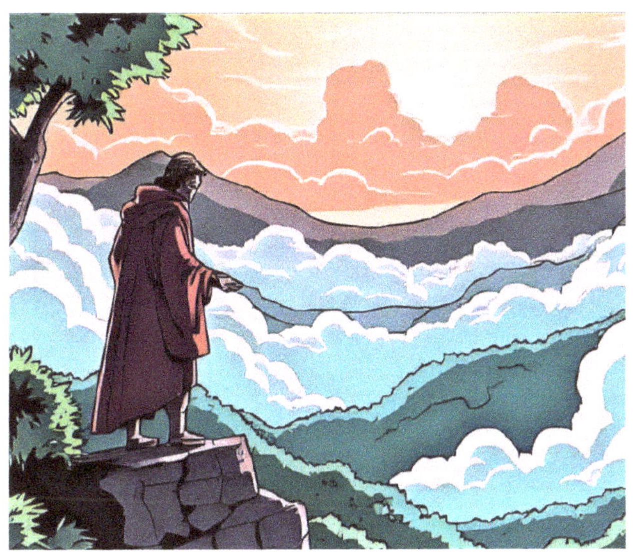

Panic

the Green Monster
likes it when I
drink and loves it
when I brood just
like Narcissus

the price of ecstasy
is life in Time
ergo the dilemma

all will be right
when the alchemist
makes his
transformation

"I was speaking of the
murdered goddess in my heart"

intellects kept underground
won't panic when
the wall comes down

Bridge in the Flood

as long as
my life is
a monster
of fate
I'll wait

"the last Poet
blew up the Word
with a Bridge
in the Flood"

("is that enough
for you Morrison")

so the ghost
followed me
to the bar
and told me
to walk which
of course made
walking an
impossibility

"the indians made me do it"

Opera Eulogy

my friend said

"it's only the
wind that rustles
the leaves"

the border where
the vigil meets
the town

Love at the
desk maintains
the rest
surrounds

the end of history
a great opera eulogy

the unlighted star

somewhere between
a promise & a
scar where the
world was created

survived Death
through the promise
now there's
no free will

to drink the
whole Western
River for the
blessèd consummation

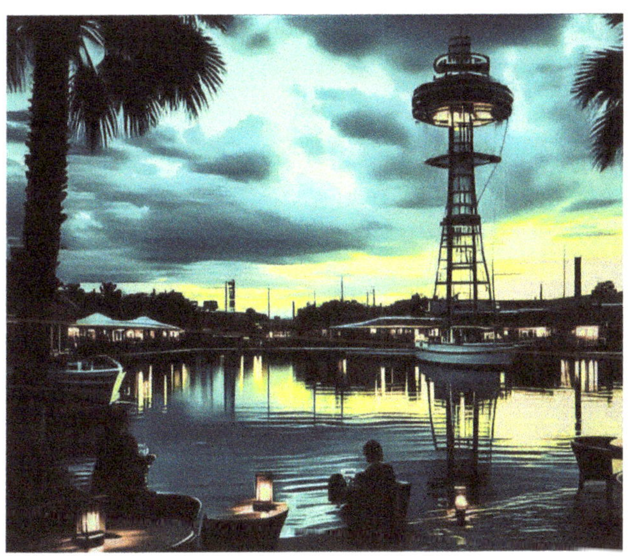

Penance and Unpeace

we promised to
obey conscience at
every turn and
overshot the goal
in monkhood reeling
backwards lunacy

to hold the cup
and not drink
waiting for the
proper angle
of alignment

these ghosts seem
adamant I'll
be paid for
these stories

destiny
intervenes
I drink

"that there powdered flesh of
heifer is what we like to call
back home 'The Temple;' you
don't go there without your
good wits about you son"

and to lose
your comfortable
view from the
bleachers on
the bandstand

my achilles
heel always
planning for
infinity

every moment
another moment
of penance
and unpeace
from which
the bread
is extracted

lost in dreams of waiting

out there is
fire and water
in here is
land so we
wait for the wind

Form Divine

screaming eagle
coat of arms

trolls in the tomb
were dressed up
in masks that showed
my bad side

let the boy's raw
heart ripen into the
            Form
            Divine
it's a feat
        (but do it blind)

Stoic Postured

on the lake
that's higher
walk around
the lake
   of fire

   "courting light by
    saving darkness"

they pushed him
off the tight rope
so he got back up
and did it again
all the way to the
shore stoic postured

to come stumbling out
of a plane crash and be
slapped in the face
with economics

then the visceral wine press

Ani Anam Ra

it takes a lot
of unknown time
& work & pains
to bring the kids
into the Temple
of Ani Anam Ra

but I'm in love
with this strange
delusion and this
anemic boredom

waiting for the
shooting star

I always needed
the mountain air

Alchemical Premise

the Science of Symbols

    (good old Orc
     nailed to the mountain
     and screaming)

the jealous nightmare
turned into armor
which lacks its comfort

it's not a love
story it's an
alchemical premise
of golden blood

desperate entanglements
can't deflect the vanity

the foolish virgin
is in the tent
draped with darkness
that's drawn
by a breeze

Cascade

this satyr leads me
through the woods
and we go fast

but every time I
see the new horizon
the green bough
of a sapling
snaps back in
my face I stop

*   *   *

the night you were exiled
in bed with a book
the Green Earth spoke
in a cascade of Ages

it felt like incense
tasted like the sea
the vigil was an
          obsidian moon

Wander Still

a trumpet sounds the
sadness wrapped in
the clairvoyance of
this way of life is
about to end in
      panoramic
      frenzy

the progress of man
a house of cards
against the Angel of
      Death
blindfolded in laurels

the New Age thundering
behind those clouds
ignored below &
      on the left

the arrogant notions of
time Eternity sheds its
skin the realness of
it will do the deed

the vagabonds
will wander still

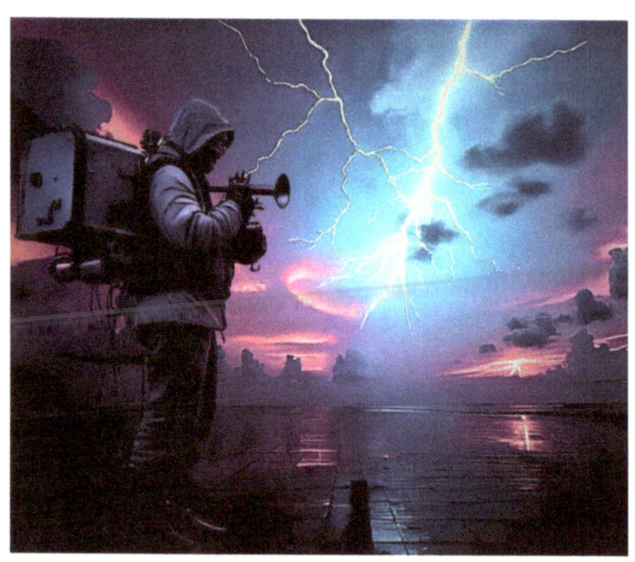

The Station

hide for so long
you forget you're
hiding and there's
the station

tried to will the
dawn with arithmetic
it almost worked
       &
Fate gave me a
hangover even
though I didn't drink

     "safe & damned"

such wariness under
camera we've won
yet the battle
goes on below

the horrible arguments
with conscience but
she wrapped my senses
in sublime repose

"things are happening
   as they must did
   you think it would
   be easy, mastering
   your fate?"

"that strength that
   feast freedom I've
   pined for since
   first awareness"

take a picture
of ecstasy as
the flesh
regenerates
dying child
miraculous cure

Pull the Strings

I did what my
Maker bid me the
rest who knows

geometry of the
Law imposed on
the plane of time

the boy knew to
take the long way
out as the house
burned down
around him

    the science of eruption
    waiting for commands

it's amazing how the
stars pull the strings
I always tried so hard

I surrender
whatever it means
I believe
in the dream

pleasure rips a hole
in the roof of this
somber enclosement
48

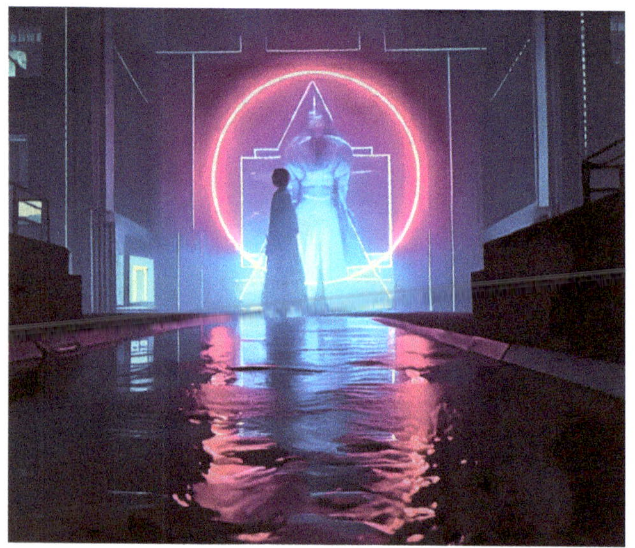

Vertigo

ruler of the waters
can't pay attention
you have to be in
form for the burial

I could hear the
fading ghost perfect
even though it
was muffled by
my own tired voice

      "wake no more
        rest before labor"

the Legend is real
I invented an island
it's just the vertigo

      "sacred ease there"

it's slow and
it hurts but
  it's love

What Is Prayer

prayer is: having
scruples stopping
       thinking

"it is what it
was wont to be"
the troubled
hero said

a wall of wind
wouldn't let me
flow so I
blamed myself

so drink tea
& say prayers

What Is Poetry

Poetry is the History
of Human Experience
(The Physics of
the Nervous System)

"Edward Scissorhands
in the American suburbs
that's a great time"
Adonis says

Adam's ascent to Eden some
kind of romantic horror flick

(*sirens*)

"he died in the war
so he went to the shore"

simple things give us
light which is why
the bunker's hard
to leave

"she'll blow up your
miserable life so
finish your reading"

"you can go when
your Garden's clean"
52

survey the wind
seasoned with fire

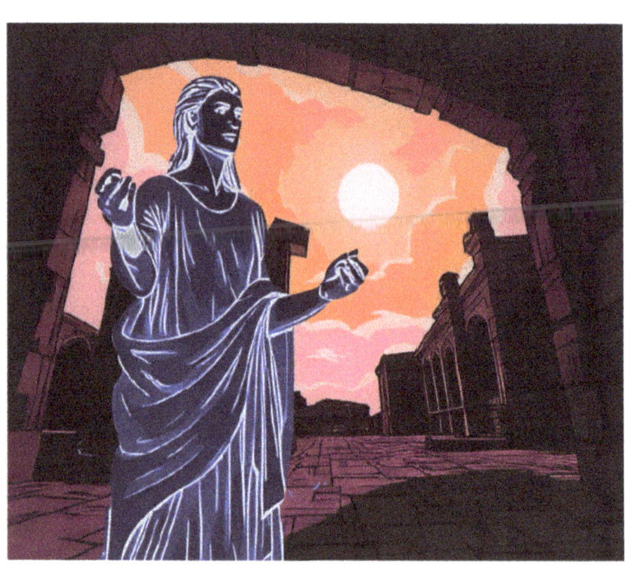

52

Detheburgher

inverted neo-
primitive (converted)

dressed up as scapegoat

"give me industrial
strength paint thinner"
says the first-century
christian martyr

I burned the paper bridges
now it's just hope & dread

afraid of the strangers
and afraid to be a
stranger
          detheburgher

to see her in
a perfect world

Naked Homer

cool people living in the ruins
feudalism is where it's at
I've ousted so many demons
when the cure eludes me
what a horrible coma
naked beggar Homer
bailing out in the streets

yesterday lava burned my eyes
I guess that's what I get
for living in a forbidden realm

    (sensory deprivation
    makes a black hole —
    you can time travel
    you *must* time travel)

the art of listening
to every burp and
whisper of conscience
especially when it's
definitively irrational

what else were
you going to do
in this world

Venusian Ovens

"Incubating is an incubus
and they come from the
same Latin etymology."

they already
read our Fate
and I wrote
all the truths

it's just my
conscience
choking my
heart again

"My heart's made of
brass. It's been through
the Venusian ovens."

the whole nation was
in danger if we
crossed the border
without first
planting the seed

Good Old Orc

trying to teach this
weird swamp creature
it's OK to mate

(architecture of the
ark — the hipster's
          morality)

lust and youth
and sanity were
missing and
replaced by the
paranormal

          he's so cold
          he makes it snow
          good old Orc
          nailed to the mountain
          and screaming —

the canned heat
          soliloquy

transfer to the
bridal chamber

Before They Spoke

it's sad outside
the hole but a
welcome change

the emotion comes
back but needs to
be soaked in brine

      "in this Gnostic text
      they tell the tale of
      when Christ tried to
      leave the tomb with
      a busted femur. it
      did not work out well"

strange skies at
the border town
withholding me from
the quiet office

      "god it's true the holy
      child doesn't know the Age
      and gets beaten for
      worshipping; I really
      believe I make all this up"

when I'm bored
even of the
dark we can
hear the ghosts
before they spoke

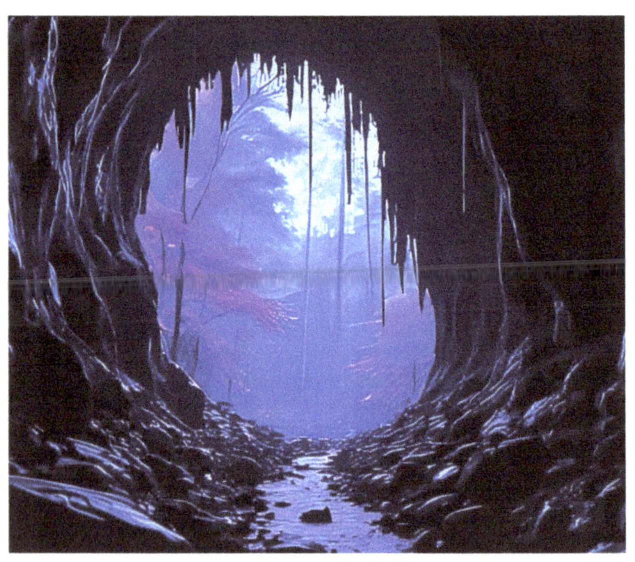

Black Crystal Foliage

I found the opening
to the cavern and
my forest still exists

the devil makes me
hate myself for the
pre-destined winds
the whim to go right

you were working
while sleepwalking

sleep deprivation
Penelopean patience

"I think the Big Fella's
happy so He's sending
visions of black crystal
foliage nightlife in the
wet dream future"

Desertion

it's the regret of not
living the life that was
stolen which is the
regret of not having regrets.

in the waking world
the beautiful scene
is the blue wine

poets will do
for the child

and close encounters
with desertion between

Make You Stop

the magic isn't
killed by darkness

how could you not
want to be alone

there was a phantom
gargoyle who always
said "you should have
done that now you
fucked up your fate"

to make brooding potent

archaic ramblings and
neo-classical monstrosities

it should make you stop
and see the stars

More Climes

after surviving the
Golden Age
Love torture —
solitude and a
mirage of leaving

> "well, at least if
>   I'm ruined waiting
>   I'll still be myself"

since it always feels like
we've been in hell forever
the temptation is that now
must be *the time* but once
our attempts at life are
sabotaged by conscience
we fall back realizing we
were still traversing more
climes of obscure death.

"when can this end"

"sobriety" said
the magic book

From the Starship

dialogue from the starship
"futurist semantics of course"

subdued by tears but not
slovenly impatience

once again nausea from
waiting pops the vein
neglecting my life with
this cadaverous drunk
(to raise a wall of vision)

"It all comes back to the
Egyptian calendar and good sex"

the boy's tired and I'm making
this border transaction — quiet
tension of the lunar realm

the city no longer in jeopardy
I'll pack this vigil in a trunk

Ghost Symmetry

the lean hours
when grief
is assuaged —

the grounds the
ghost didn't stomp

my heart is
wandering somewhere
and somehow
thunderbolts of shame

if Death were
an equation of
golden symmetry
it'd look pretty
       silly

Bad Epiphanies

I could hear the
soundtrack of my
climax before I
died

    (defying gravity)

these inane miracles
squeezing me like
    the wine press

*   *   *

"How's Golgonooza treating you
Looney Tunes?"

"Hello. Hello. Dumb hick on line 3.
My name's Billy."

"I'll be your girlfriend Billy," says
the Blue Whore

"O God," he says and saunters
away with bad epiphanies and
ugly masculine contortions

"Saw a Shakespearean rape
scene in NYC" whiskeylips
told the ghost

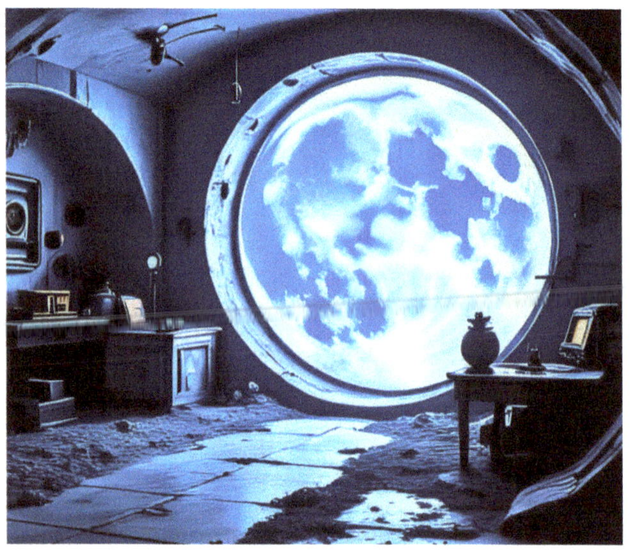

Like Neuroses

"Leash of the Cadaver
  Land of Ill-Repute"

    (he's got a goat
    heart that beats
    like neuroses)

"I know there are plenty of
hot spots left on this planet"

cobwebs on the ceiling
of the sky are painted
blue, to match the womb
of the moon with the
vertigo of weightlessness
in the room that's a tomb

"to make two sexes they
both had to be crippled
somehow, didn't they"

"Pick on someone your own size"

"Ha ha ha ha ha"

Tentacles

I said all my prayers
now they won't write
me a new prescription

walked through the country
to the town and dropped
dead in the bedlam of vanity

ego portal on the
other side of the black
hole complete with
night tentacles

Was Real

I watch the scar
get smaller, but
sometimes that
plundered dead
monk was real
and we're still
trying to learn
how to live
every day

but I love to cling
this forlorn rosary

O the horrible
custody battles —

just another bored
lifetime of immortality
for this satyr so
he doesn't let
me have any fun

large eyes unfurl
the wasteland in
a camera lens

Soothsayer

"where is he?"
the fire says

I retort, unafraid

"with the blind sooth-
sayer at a boar sacrifice"
as if it weren't
quite vacant enough

"we crossed the leprous
pit of impure youth
and I feel like
myself what a novelty"

the ghost follows
me to the bar
       again

(the stuff the
senses refract)

blessings in disguise
while bloodletting —
active-passive
     right of way

"One arrival wasn't
enough . . . insane
otherworldly obligations
. . . what misery my
life and truth have
been boiling in my
skull for so long
because these opaque
concubines won't leave
me alone"

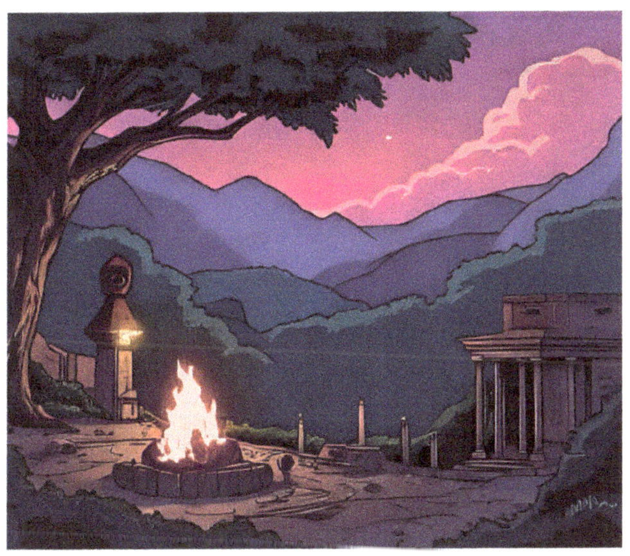

Avoiding Destruction

the pain without horror
that beats me to life

all the poetry and
spirituals love sincerity
couldn't save the mouse
from avoiding destruction

so he put on
monk's robes
and looked away
to learn the lie

the boy choked
the man found
sawdust in a
frugal office

Blue assed Baboon

"I met a falling victim
and was unafraid. It's
just the kids who fall
can't help save the
world."

"In the fiery pits of
Golgonooza we like to
call that a blue-assed
baboon"

the tree a
corpse a
schizophrenic
virgin the
flood dogs
ghosts
movies

I saw the pillar then, of course
you know, fell back again

to come stumbling
out of a plane crash
and be slapped in
the face with economics

A Flag of Vision

this beautiful young
man who's been sitting
here biting his tongue
with a hole in his side

"I'm a lot like everybody
except I'm not a hypocrite"
he says

we locked the Garden gates
until the bell was cast

my "corpse"
drawn and quartered
from the Pyramids
to this foul waste —
R.J. Waldendörf
Collected Poems

they won't write
me a prescription
because I said
all my prayers
waiting for a
new realm of
blood to raise

a flag of vision
but I'm too
good at suffering
poor crippled
heart

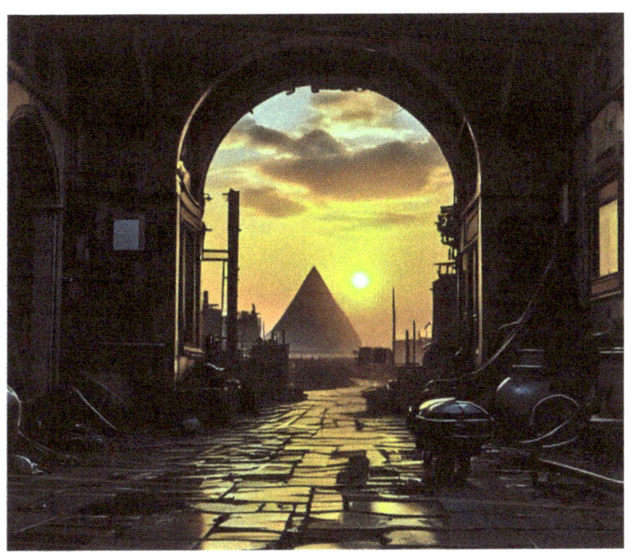

Our Lady

all those days of fever
and you came and pacified
me before the glaciers
could pulverize my bones
Our Lady's heart survived
by the sovereign writer

those cave paintings on
my nervous system that
led me away to safe
    damnation

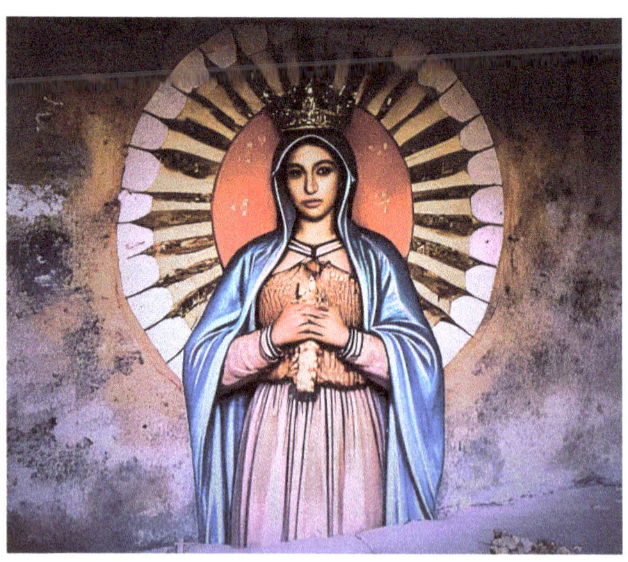

Diagrams

"fishing for trout in the
wrong stream" my newest
vision of bondage

I toured the town
saw nothing but a
wall posted with
diagrams of these
unhealed injuries —
but the Voice (that's
become me) promised
a reasonable way
of life one day

the funny thing is the
unborn chicken voices
were in my head so now
I pull their puppet strings

Organic Arpanet

our organic Arpanet
never crashed

they wave anachronistic
flags they found in a
barn and demand
total submission

"Evolution doesn't happen fast
enough. That's it: dumb Nature"

"Are you implying a simian holocaust"

"exactly"

I made this
dumb hill a
mystic abode
what a feat

Weird Arena

injuries made this dumb
flesh love the desolate
repose

      but don't lie you love this
      self-contained masculine
      violence and the fiery
      pits of Golgonooza burning
      the phoenix by hiding
      from women

you knew how
long it would take
to come back

strange autumnal corridor
a weird arena of birth

Far Gone

waiting for the worst
to end and saw
canned heat on the
shelf so drank the

           dregs

"I bet there's a corpse a corridor
and a film behind door number three"

"horse's ass in
the hollow tree
blah bluh blah
bluh blah"

the storms at sea
that made me sick
and the severity —
no wonder you're
so alone, so far gone

Burnished Arm

she chose
chastity because
love was not
there so I
built the bower
before she
was born

the hipster's morality
a psychological thriller —

because there's a
door in the wall
that a goddess
   opens

combative ego re-
appearance at the
city limits my
burnished arm
reclined

Lazarus becomes erect
grace before fish

A New Scourge

sit around
and wait for
a ridiculous
fate

the devil tries
out a new
scourge

what a miracle
to watch the
wind lift the
death fog

there's a strange
expression watching
the partisans quarrel

Condemned

the stars are
watching me in
this dumb canyon

light contrives
with darkness

teeth grow

the gravedigger
moseys on stage
pockets in hands
"this place needs
to be condemned"

blindness cured at
a deserted boardwalk

then this obsequious
effeminate troll
brings me a new
plague from Time

Eclipse

he takes
the risk of
waiting for
eclipse

let the cat wait

checkpoints give
back the watch
when they pull
back the leash
with a plague

"that's the Tao of
tangy trout bergurs,
sir . . . er . . . madam"

Same Bloody Sun

"they are dead
in a hill and
I am not even
born" is the
prophylactic

Golgotha was
an amusement
park under the
same bloody sun

in Dionysus'
nightmare

Water Hydraulics

once in love
with misery
rising seeking
bottom like
water hydraulics

the innocent
larva can't
imagine wings

with the brake
on his voice

spiritual
reproduction
procedures —

the blue tent
of non-being
   &
magma amoebas

Blue Christmas Lights

the devil's
dues keep
disasters away

the Movie can
begin when the
child stops
believing in
clouds — that
are the lies
of ghosts

then tents in an
abandoned city

blue christmas lights
germinate in the mummy

I saw ghosts
of folly that
never was as
I crossed the
bridge —

he escaped in
a windless valley

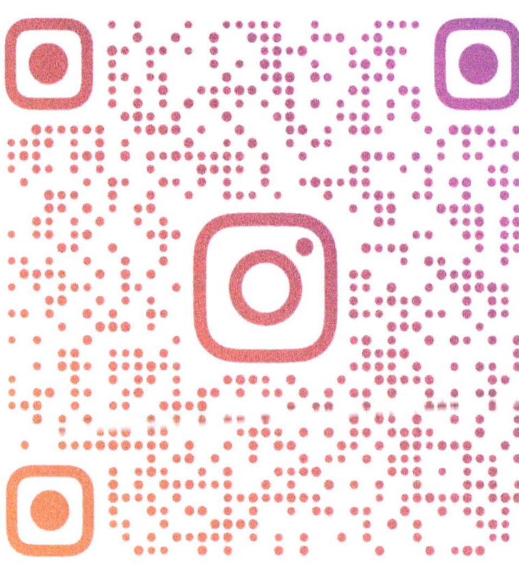

TABBOTTCOLLINS

About the Author

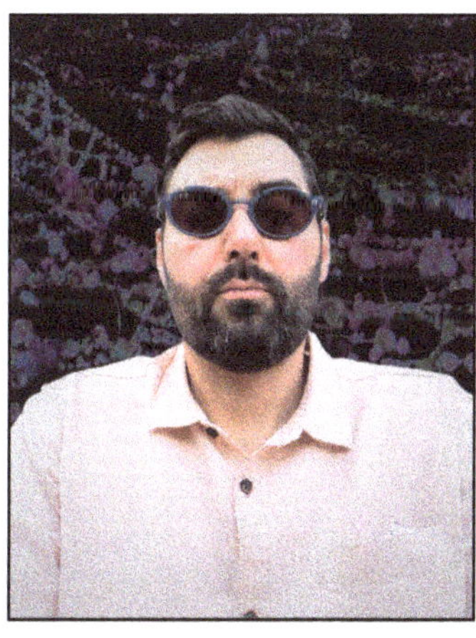

T. Abbott Collins has published poems in small literary journals since 2011. He released an experimental rap album under the moniker looCcaM in 2023. *Apocalyptic Clichés*, his first collection of poems, was published in 2024 by Fifth Entelechy Publishing, an imprint he established. His poetic style draws influence from the Anglo-American and European avant-garde traditions of the 20th century and is grounded in catachresis, fragmentation, ellipsis, and dense imagery: It is a poetics of miniaturization and plasticity. Tim, as known by family and friends, has also published scholarly articles on metaphor and sound in poetry, and more specifically on the work of Chaucer, Poe, Wu-Tang Clan, Jean Baudrillard and Jacques Lacan. He worked for several years as an adjunct instructor and has been working as an unwaged researcher and poet for many years. Tim plans to release four more volumes of poems and has begun work on a novel. This collection was composed between 2004 and 2008.